Facts About the Oystercatcher

By Lisa Strattin

© 2016 Lisa Strattin

Revised © 2019

Facts for Kids Picture Books by Lisa Strattin

Harlequin Macaw, Vol 34

Downy Woodpecker, Vol 37

Frilled Lizard, Vol 39

Purple Finch, Vol 48

Poison Dart Frogs, Vol 50

Giant Otter, Vol 57

Hornbill, Vol 67

Dwarf Lemur, Vol 73

Giant Squirrel, Vol 76

Star Tortoise, Vol 79

Sign Up for New Release Emails Here

http://LisaStrattin.com/subscribe-here

Monthly Surprise Box

http://KidCraftsByLisa.com

Contents

INTRODUCTION

The oystercatcher is a large bird that can be found on ocean shorelines and in salty marshlands. It gets its name from the fact that its diet is largely made up of oysters, though it also eats mussels and clams, among other small animals commonly found on beaches.

There are many species of oystercatchers that live all around the world, except the North and South poles. Two species of oystercatchers are native to the United States: the American oystercatcher, which lives on the east coast, along the Gulf of Mexico, and into the Caribbean Islands, and the black oystercatcher, which lives along the west coast of California, Oregon, Washington State, and Alaska.

CHARACTERISTICS

Because of how they hunt, oystercatchers tend to walk or run, rather than fly. They like to walk along parts of the beach where there are lots of oysters. When they see an oyster with its shell partly open, they'll jab their sharp beak inside in order to get at the meat.

While they tend to walk a lot of the time, oystercatchers can also fly and swim. In fact, they are known to dive into the ocean in order to escape other predators like hawks and owls. Large young birds have been seen diving several meters deep. They can use their wings to swim under water for nearly thirty feet. When they feel safe, they return to the surface and swim atop the water, like a duck.

Like many birds, oystercatchers sleep with their bills tucked under their wings and spend a good deal of time preening, using their feet and bills to clean and flatten their feathers.

APPEARANCE

The American oystercatcher, which lives along the American shores of the Atlantic Ocean, has a black head, a brown back, and white to whitish-yellow belly. Along the Pacific, the black oystercatcher is usually as black as its name implies, though colors ranging from dark brown to dark gray are also common. Both species have conspicuously large, bright orange bills.

LIFE STAGES

Like all birds, oystercatchers are born from eggs. A nest of oystercatchers in North America typically has between one and four eggs. It takes around three to four weeks for the eggs to hatch. Both the mother and father bird take turns incubating the nest, which means they sit on top of it in order to keep the eggs warm. In warmer climates, where the eggs may get too hot, the adults will also use their bodies to provide shade for their nest.

When the eggs hatch, the young birds are covered in downy feathers, and are unable to fly for the first five weeks of their life. Because their nests are built on the ground, however, chicks are able to leave it soon after they hatch and walk around.

Both parents share the chore of feeding their young for as long as two months, though young birds often begin feeding themselves well before their parents stop bringing them food.

When they are three to four years old, oystercatchers will find a mate that they will often keep for life.

LIFE SPAN

The oldest oystercatcher was known to be nearly twenty-four-years-old, though in the wild they likely don't live to be nearly so old. This is because in the wild they must face predators, and sometimes suffer from lack of food or water.

SIZE

At nearly two feet long and with a wingspan as long as three feet, the oystercatchers are relatively large birds.

HABITAT

The American oystercatcher, along the east coast of the United States, lives on sandy beaches or tidal mudflats. Other than staying near the ocean, precisely where they live depends largely on the availability of food.

Like their eastern cousins, where black oystercatchers live is largely determined by the presence of food. In contrast to American oystercatchers, however, black oystercatchers prefer rocky over sandy beaches.

Both species can also be found on islands not far from the mainland, where there tend to be fewer predators to threaten them.

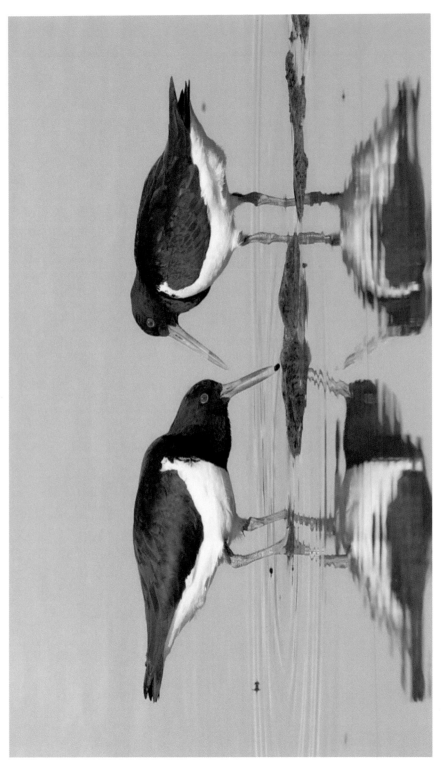

DIET

As their name implies, oystercatchers find and eat oysters!

They also eat other bivalve animals, that is, animals whose shells are made of two halves, with a hinge that can open between them like a door, such as clams and mollusks.

In addition, some oystercatchers eat worms, crabs, and fish. In fact, different kinds of oystercatchers have differently shaped bills, depending on which food they prefer, narrower, pointier bills are used to probe the mud and sand for buried food. Flatter, more knife-like bills are more often used to hunt for oysters and clams.

FRIENDS AND ENEMIES

An oystercatcher's neighbors would be other shore-bound birds, such as seagulls, flamingos, plovers, and sometimes geese.

Its enemies include other, predatory birds such as owls, eagles, and hawks, as well dogs and cats, foxes, skunks, coyotes and bobcats.

If a nest is approached by a predator, oystercatchers, like many birds, will attempt to distract the predator away. They will do this by first slipping away from the nest, hopefully unseen, while the predator is still some distance away. They will then allow themselves to be seen, sometimes fluttering near the ground and giving distress calls, pretending to be injured. This is to get the predator to move away from the nest.

Adults protecting their nests will also pretend to sleep out in the open, where predators can see them. When approached, and sometimes approached so closely that they are even touched, by a predator, they will then fly or run to someplace nearby, where they will again pretend to sleep. They will do this again and again, leading the predator farther and farther away from their nest.

SUITABILITY AS PETS

While some birds make great pets, given their size, the volume of their calls, which are described as peeps and weeps, as well as their dietary and habitat needs, oystercatchers probably wouldn't do very well caged in a house. Imagine every day feeding a large bird many, many oysters, which would smell strongly like tuna fish and leave stinky shells in the bottom of the cage!

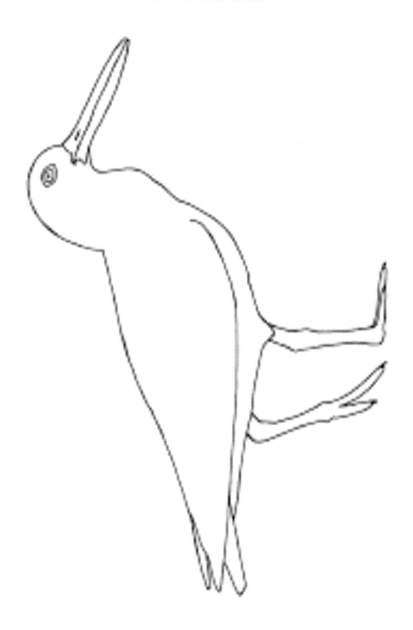

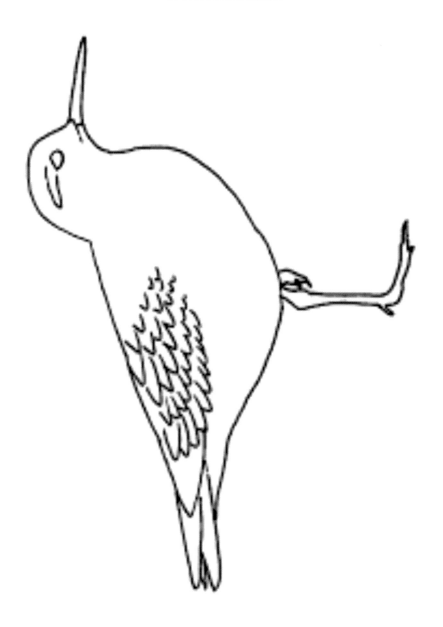

COLOR ME

COLOR ME

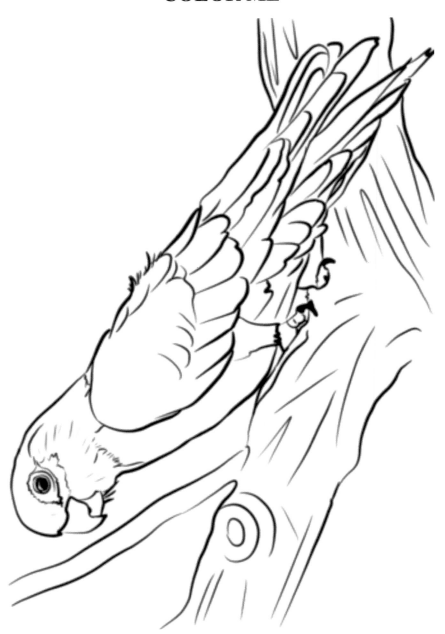

COLOR ME

COLOR ME

Please leave me a review here:

http://lisastrattin.com/Review-Vol-127

For more Kindle Downloads Visit Lisa Strattin Author Page on Amazon Author Central

http://amazon.com/author/lisastrattin

To see upcoming titles, visit my website at LisaStrattin.com– all books available on kindle!

http://lisastrattin.com

OYSTERCATCHER PUZZLE

You can get one by copying and pasting this link into your browser:

http://lisastrattin.com/oystercatcherpuzzle

MONTHLY SURPRISE BOX

Get yours by copying and pasting this link into your browser

http://KidCraftsByLisa.com

Printed in Great Britain
by Amazon

80639132R00022